THE
WORKING
CLASSIC

Aaron Kent

Published 2023 by the87press
The 87 Press LTD
87 Stonecot Hill
Sutton
Surrey
SM3 9HJ
www.the87press.co.uk

ISBN: 978-1-7393939-1-5

Printed and bound by CPI Group (UK) Ltd, Croydon, CR0 4YY
Design: Stanislava Stoilova [www.sdesign.graphics]

Rise with your class, not out of it.
— John MacLean

This body of poems, fictional interviews and reviews sees Aaron Kent target social inequality through a shuffling of reality. The moon is arrested for non-violent protest while one defiant speaker declares 'I am sometimes a song'. The legion of alternative selves here are resourceful, prepared to 'Instrument the silence' and reveal 'the amount of light in an ending'. The results are spectacular, classism and gentrification exposed from a dynamic array of angles. Ferocious, intimate, important.

—John McCullough, *Panic Response*

To wake from the simulation that seems to equate its power with surcease. Aaron Kent's *The Working Classic* can be nothing other than existential kinetic as neo-renewal as liberation from the class stamped rigidities of generational inbred British boundedness.

—Will Alexander, *Refractive Africa*

A definite classic; Kent continues to find new words and new forms to peel back the layers of the self. Non-linear, unpredictable and always surprising, this is a book only Kent could conceive of , and certainly one that nobody else could write.

—Andrew McMillan, *100 Queer Poems* (co-editor)

There are books that UK poetry needs, and there are books that UK poetry deserves. Needs, like the salvation of its soul. Deserves, like a smack in the face with a Millwall brick. The Working Classic is both. It is, amongst other things, an incisive and playful engagement with what poetry is, to whom it belongs, and with the endless orgy of mind-numbing waffle that surrounds its publication and reception. It is satirically sharp, genuinely insightful, and often hilarious.

More than this, Aaron Kent is a candid and nuanced chronicler of what it means to be working class in the twenty-first century. That is, to be irrevocably, painfully, and marvellously shaped by class; classed in our engagement with language and literary culture; in our encounters with each other and the world. The Working Classic is full of coruscating verbal parries, beautifully off kilter image-making, and moments of pained, serrated tenderness. It recognises and holds us, but with an eye and in a voice that is entirely its own.

I don't doubt that The Working Classic will alienate and vex a number of people. It should. That's what good writing is for.

—Fran Lock, *White/Other*

Foreword
By Antony Owen

Some years ago, my uncle took me for a walk off the public path above a mountain above Penmaenmawr to a derelict outhouse near an old quarry. Inside this outhouse was a slim window without a pane, what filled it was a split screen of sea and sky plus a bird accepting the thermals then disappearing like a comma against a poem by Anon. When I was less than halfway through reading *The Working Classic* I was deluged with memories like this that connected me to tiny squared mosaics that made up the broken Roman floor of who we are in all our glory and fading. To read *The Working Classic* is a narcotic experience of feeling the narrative protagonist-centric poems as much as reading them. You root for the people because despite singular characterisations there is a universal sense of mutual displacement in the world we live in. If you are working-class then your social expectations would draw a diagram of people looking up not at an even level of standing. Aaron Kent is incredibly adept at redefining and deconstructing stigma of what working-class looks like. Is it a grizzled man with a small sharp pencil tucked into *his* ear banging bumps out of metal sheets? Is it a scrawny miner with an ailing canary billowing in a cage emerging from the heart of a Welsh field? In short no, it really is not. Is it a human being on a Trident submarine the length of Big Ben who is avoiding danger within the submarine in the unmapped waters of unflagged sea trying to find his true north? Is it a stickman from a Lowry painting jumping out and you see a human face and the contorted map of a life you piece together because you've read *The Working Classic*? Yes, in short it is. An example of this is in one of the poem extracts below that *will find you* as you work your way through the unmapped territories of working-class writing that have not been written in this way before because let me be clear on this:

1

Aaron Kent is no emulator of concrete poems or prose. Such is Aaron Kent's originality his work does not remind me of any other poet writing today whether working-class, political or otherwise like those who still muse about issues as pressing as the smell of books in Wordsworth's cottage. His poems in *The Working Classic* are epic miniatures of people who are like the old stories in stone against the gleaming commissioned marble in a church laden with gold in a neglected community. Kent explores the placement of the overlooked here:

This house is a box in a city of boxes .

> Inside of both myself and the house, there's a broken glass jar so dark that I can weep into its echo. We let the universe open into silence, an effigy, a shape growing slowly from the cupped hands of an ash tree. The bridge hangs from laburnum, their drops a sweet, deadly liquorice. I wouldn't have met this thing had I not been so close to being and/or do. If I can speak inside the flesh of a flower, I still love you now and suddenly, this is just the unpeeling of a single layer of skin and paint at the edge of a wasteland

I think *The Working Classic* is unplugged poetry. It is a musical language at its most natural in that it exists as an opus of fully intentional assonance and discordance that is beautiful to hear, comfortable to listen to, uncomfortable to hear and where the sound a spilt chord is the poetry and not the manufactured Frankenstein of what middle-class writers marionetting imagined working-class experiences want to be. The intensity and beauty of Aaron Kent's writing is much like some Japanese poets I admire where there is a detachment of drama and attachment only to the human coping mechanism of existing in natural and unnatural environs. Much of the soul that sage-smokes out from Kent's books are the physical and psychological challenges we face as people. Going back to the skilful expressive stoicism of Japanese poets (particularly the Hibakusha poets) Kent is someone who articulates abrupt changes whether that is his body wiped out like the wood and paper houses of Hiroshima or the alpha male/human conflict men find themselves in day to day at work, in relationships etc.

The Working Classic is intimate, courageous and deeply affecting to the point I created a repository of emotions that left me a more complete person for ~~reading experiencing~~ absorbing it. We have a new wave of working-class writers in the UK that are all infinitely different and creating the burn in that tug-o-war where poetry should belong. On one side is a rope of burning horsehair and the other a velvet cord which is not allowed to be touched by dirty hands.

Some living working-classic poets you will have to look really hard to find are:

Owen Gallagher, Martin Hayes, Katy Wareham-Morris, Peter Raynard, Emma Purshouse, Nail Fulwood, Neil Young, Umberto Lienzi, Nryains Plealoo, Joseph Horgan

Imagine what he could've done if he'd used his
MAXIMUM HEADROOM
(Kent, *All English Wank*, 2022)

Whenever I forget what AI is,
I ask myself what my primary school teacher would say.
He'd whip his shirt off several times a lesson
so we could all watch him make his pecs dance.
Wait a minute, this was supposed to be a poem,
I forgot to include all the poetry and whatnot.
All the bits about the flowers catching the morning sun
reflecting off the back of a lake's shimmering mystery.
The definitive reason for existence that of watching
a bee collect enough pollen to have itself killed.
In hindsight, there's too many poems that exist to be poems,
too many PE teachers tensing their chests for meagre applause.

To be unknowing as though to be a ghost
(Kent, *Colonel Mustard's Spectacular Trick Candelabra*, 2019)

Sickly sweet, I should have said
that I am sometimes a song. A song
of ice and a forest of cedars.

I should have asked you to come
at me with a gun in my mouth
in a bed a mile from all I've known.

I'm sorry I failed to mention
I cannot sleep when I breathe you out.
Whenever you touch my cheek I die.

The Moon is Being Arrested for Non-violent Protest
(Kent, *Integrated Bowel Syndrome*, 2018)

Sometimes it's better to feel nothing but
the love, for some people, that I can't
be more than: a heart that isn't as big
as it should be. I've made love to the moon
and the sky – it put some distance between

my body and the world.
One person can be both
an eight ball of sugary sweets
and the dust that fills a room –
I'm glad to find you in myself.

I ain't got the time to care
about no double negatives,
or not. When they complain
about being fined to go on holiday,
I remind them there are kids living

in craters on far-off dwarf planets.
I can hear the sound of my blood
travelling through the weather's veins.
Ha! Weathervane, get it? I am in the dark,
but you've seen the heart of the room.

This house is a box in a city of boxes
(Kent, *Map of a House Nobody Asked for*, 2020)

its eaves burnt down to a black pearl, so it could lie down in more than stone. It is a cat's claws that move across my face. We take it in turns to discard out joy, to exacerbate our laughs as we dream inside individual thoughts. I cannot remember its former shape, and resort to drawing a fire towards the sky. Inside of both myself and the house, there's a broken glass jar so dark that I can weep into its echo. We let the universe open into silence, an effigy, a shape growing slowly from the cupped hands of an ash tree. The bridge hangs from laburnum, their drops a sweet, deadly liquorice. I wouldn't have met this thing had I not been so close to being and/or do. If I can speak inside the flesh of a flower, *I still love you now and suddenly*, this is just the unpeeling of a single layer of skin and paint at the edge of a wasteland. We are one house between latticed perimeters, old, tumbling down over itself, pulling out grey fruit. The garden a complete infinity passing through windows and spinning stars. It is empty, but outside, there are scraps of cloth that gleam against the ruin. The interior is always moving outside of me, darkening, pulling out the dead, whispering in the cracked walls, the magma pools. The life of a renaissance artist inside of a nightmare they've drawn.

It would take so little from one side of the world to the other
(Kent, *Guide to Nightlife*, 2018)

And the man on the bridge was me
a hundred miles away,
the waves like ice cream,
the waves like a place to stay forever.
      As an adult all is illusion.

When I was sixteen
I lost the ability to read
tsunamis and their irreparable
lessons. It left me like tap-water.

I realised I couldn't put back
my sink, my toilet, the windows.
      No matter, I am too toxic to cry.

My childhood dangled
like toothpicks and callouses,
I half ran away in my sleep
to handstand off the roof
and drown in rushes of loss.

Aaron Kent, The Art of Poetry No. 101

Interviewed by Amik Ron   Issue 218, Fall 2016

'I'm deathly allergic to horses,' Aaron Kent warns me as I step into his spare bedroom to interview him. The warning seems irrelevant, I hadn't brought a horse into his house, and there didn't seem to be a reason why I would have. 'I found out when I went to a horse sanctuary and touched every single horse there. My face swelled, throat tightened, eyes closed over. I had to get to A&E as soon as possible.' I ask Kent why he is sharing this story, but he shakes his head and asks me to follow him to the living room. It makes a change from him sharing the story of his brain haemorrhage again.[1]

There, in front of a large black bookcase, Aaron runs his fingers over the books, 'I don't really do interviews, but I read that sharing weaknesses humanises you, makes the reader like you.' His book shelf seems to have several sections: just Jacques Cousteau, favourite poetry books, books to be read, stuff he has published as an editor, stuff he has had published as a poet. He finally offers me a drink before we begin the interview.

INTERVIEWER

I've always got the impression that you aren't really sure of the type of poet you want to be. Your genre of poetry switches a lot.

---

[1] I hadn't sustained a brain haemorrhage (2020) until a year after the writing of this interview (2019), a year before writing this footnote (2021), three years before the publication of this book (2023).

AARON

I guess that's a fair assessment, I mean I probably wouldn't write my debut *Colonel Mustard's Spectacular Trick Candelabra* again, but I don't know how many people would, I mean, we're all growing right? I had gone for a sort of visual approach in a way, to kind of use cheap tricks as this stylistic thing to make people like the work. If you dig in, it's not actually any good. Like, that 'unknowing ghost' poem has the line 'A song / of ice and a forest of cedars' which is way too close to that whole Game of Thrones series with, I think this is correct, *A song of Ice and Fire*. I've not read the books, they're not really my thing, but my ideas clearly aren't that good if large chunks of them have some sort of subconscious commercial undertone, right? I dunno, early work is early work, it's all just discovering where you are and what you want. Not that later work isn't that too, but later work doesn't get you jacked off by the elites for *debut prizes*.

INTERVIEWER

Do you think you have become more certain of your place in the world as a pansexual, working-class writer?

AARON

You could say that, or you could say I got bored of not being allowed to be me. People would judge me because I say 'ain't' or because I use a glottal stop, or because of my upbringing and the area I grew up in. And I used to try to hide that, and to pronounce 'th' as 'th' rather than 'f' or 'v', but in the end that wasn't me. I heard politicians using that sort of speech to appeal to the regular person, and poets who changed the way they spoke to sound 'street' in spite of their privilege and the fact their rich-ass parents paid for them to go to some elite private performance academy, and I thought *fuck it, if the upper class can use my voice to put me two steps back and themselves two steps forward, then I'll just buy into it and be me.* You know?

INTERVIEWER
There's the double negative line in a poem in your book, in the poem titled for the moon being arrested.

AARON
Yeah, that's in my debut *Integrated Bowel Syndrome*. The follow up line on that is often overlooked for the obviousness of the double negative – so I sometimes feel like I should've taken that out.

INTERVIEWER
The follow up line is the one that references being fined for holidays while poor kids shelter in craters on far off planets?

AARON
Yeah. That's about middle-class parents complaining they were being fined for taking their kids out of school for holiday. In the grand scheme of things, the fines were relatively meagre for families that could afford to go off on expensive holidays. Like, if you're happy to sacrifice a couple weeks of your kid's education to take them to Disneyworld, or an all-inclusive jaunt to the Maldives, then you can stump up a £60 fine. At the same time, child tax credits and income support were being capped at a maximum of two children. Further children could feature on a claim, but only if they were the result of a rape. So, you've got people complaining their holiday was sixty quid extra, while benefit claimants had to sit with government officials and medical professionals to tell them about the most horrendous experiences of their lives just to keep being able to feed their kids.

INTERVIEWER

My perception of you is one of somebody who wants to write poetry but isn't entirely sure of what they're writing.

AARON

Maybe? Isn't that everybody who writes? Well, maybe not everybody, that's a weird generalisation, but surely I'm not unique in that sense. I mean, everything I write I hate afterwards, and I think that probably improves me. My debut pamphlets *Ice Skating*, *Hungarian Grandad*, and *Map of a Home Nobody Asked For* are different, sure, but I don't know if it would be entirely fair to justify that difference as coming from a lack of certainty on my side. Yeah, I don't want to read my old work anymore, and yeah, when I read new poets and better poets I suddenly realise why everything I've done is wrong, and yeah, I wonder what sort of taste anybody who would actually buy my books has.

INTERVIEWER

What are you currently working on?

AARON

(Sneezes) Sorry, must be a horse somewhere (laughs). I'm working on my debut, set to be titled *Working-class Lack* but I actually want to call it *Working-class Scum*. (Sneezes) Sorry. It started as me just writing about my working-class upbringing, and raging against the Tories, but it eventually became different, a sort of mock-autobiography about a fictionalised Aaron Kent. It's very critical towards him (sneezes), very anti-Aaron. I mean, you would know.

INTERVIEWER

You ever feel like moving on and focussing on something not class-related?

AARON

Yeah, I know. I'm going to get a lot of comments like 'get over it, you were poor,' people keep saying that. I'm trying to. I've decided I'm going to try and do two things: write some of the best poems I've ever written about the area I grew up in, and become a lawyer. If it's not the latter that I become, I'll go back to being a scumbag. But I'll become a better scumbag. (laughs)

INTERVIEWER

What if you became a lawyer but didn't like it?

AARON

I'm not going to be a lawyer. Obviously.

INTERVIEWER

You know what's actually exciting though? There's some stuff in your debut pamphlet *All English Wank* and some stuff in your debut book *Guide to Nightlife* that are genuinely fascinating, I think. How does it feel knowing that your work is more important than you're actually making out?

AARON

It feels like failure. The more you're at a disadvantage, the more self-loathing you go through. This isn't true of everyone, I'm sure, but it's one of the reasons I'm writing this book: I really don't want to feel that way again. I've just got to keep writing until I can stop feeling like that. It's hard to explain to people: I hate writing the same poems over and over. The easiest thing about writing a pamphlet is that I can continue writing pamphlets forever and it'll be perfectly fine. I might have written six pamphlets this year. And after six pamphlets of misery and self-loathing, that's when it'll happen: I won't have anything left to say, and my book will be shit, and I'll call it quits and find another way to hate myself. I guess I keep hoping that I can come up with something good to make others hate me more than I hate myself.

At this point I took off my mask and revealed myself to be a horse. Aaron almost instantly started to panic, struggling to breathe. I fled through the open door, my suspicion is his allergies are real – but he has exacerbated the impact they have on him.

Did I discover the real Aaron Kent? No. Probably not. He seems insecure, a bit cowardly, like he isn't even willing to call himself a poet. I wonder what the future holds for him, but I feel like there are two things that will be in short supply for him: literary accolades and horses.

Intrepid explorer, this whole house is a landmine
(Kent, *Sleeping with the Frenemy*, 2010)

Colossal, as if to say caught in amber and preserved along
fault lines,
as if to wake with 3 of the 4 quadrants intact. Oh remarkable us,
it has become a chore to sweep for debris, though it would
be a reach
if every investigation fell off the trawler. When there are
soldiers in the house

we become distant from those geared up for a test of weaponry –
I'd rather they bit my fingers off. There are reasons to keep a
faulty tie,
cup of tea, windchime beyond the potential for a boot-sale,
but that's the good stuff.
I remember growing up, for some reason. I would've taken
the heat off myself

and not bothered if I had this method of expression at fifteen.
I exist to teach myself something I already know, which is
The Teletubbies do not deserve to have their own TV show,
when I make coffee I wonder if caffeine shows up on an MRI.

I stopped taking the pills that made me sleep
(Kent, *The Kent Boys*, 2018)

My brother's got a broken leg,
we can't pay the rent;
I've been working at the car wash for weeks
and I still can't stop him breaking it every other day.
It works when the weather's nice,
he just wants to be alone.

I know where I'm going now,
and I know how I'll do it.
I'll show you the view from the edge
if you show me yours.

It takes no longer than three seconds
for the room to start shrinking around you
when you close your eyes and convince yourself
you're small. They'll never put our names
in the dictionary. If God was a person,
he'd be in the Book of the Dead
sitting naked on a bar stool, with a stranger –
instead, that's what I have to do,
always picking up after the big G's slack.

I can't believe He ever felt something for me.
My head's full of black and white photos
of a room and a child that I don't know.
It takes more than one pill to make it worth not waking up.
We can lie here until we go out and look for what's real.

When things get tough I imagine I am a snail experiencing the sweet relief of being crushed by a boot
(Kent, *Houses the Size of Angles*, 2020)

My poetry tries too hard to reveal the depth of my self-loathing in ways I can attune to music. It has taken me three weeks to write a sentence that exists to say I hate myself. I haven't fallen off the bed, don't worry. I'm supposed to be writing about stingrays being magnetic, 'cause even if they aren't they should be. The middle-class won't publish my poems 'cause they don't like reality, that and I don't send them poems. Who wants to read about terraced houses and free school meals when the hill's travelling light meanders in ways the salamander can but dream of. I have eaten the pithiviers the Royal Society of Literature served me, and now my parents won't allow me home, instead pointing to the 'No Class Traitors' sign. I've tried to tell Mum I didn't like the rich almond filling, that I laughed at the sight of the Pumpkin Seed Mole, that I made them all feel guilty about inviting the grandson of a refugee to a party explicitly designed to exclude us. Mum, you tapped so hard you dented the sign. I had the advantageous ineptitude of sleep to tremor the hotel room they wouldn't subsidise. There are no late nights when every morning starts with you still awake from the night before. Bedtime is just an excuse to save money on heating. The last time I properly slept I felt my brain switch off like a kettle during the adverts at half time.

Between All Of Us Like A Wavy Halo Form
(Kent, *Legitimately, I'm Sorry I Suck*, 2019)

The long river of the unconscious
        where we all are home,
tossing planets and asteroids aside.

The yawning drag of orbit
        I haven't breathed since
        I got back from Paris,
the oomph is real. The soundless

silent and the voice of the voice;
        there's little time. In time
we might have to be the first to go.

The cycle of birth and death:
        pressure, seeped in blues,
carries deep echoes of the dotcom boom
and bust. Wile E Coyote is still
        beneath the soft space
        and press back down.

The universe under our skin
        like carpet. I go in to feel
        a sound and a feel,

        crawl inside the blood
        brain/ear/brain and look
around inside the shadowy corners
with half-light and half-darkness:
three in the morning. Contrast this

        with the feel of a hand coming

out of a jacket, the sound of a hand
on a shoulder. Come close to sleep
with the heat rising off the pavement.
I am tired to the bone but I will not sleep
        for night-time is our friend.

How could I betray the earth like this?
(Kent, *A Breakfast for the Neighbours*, 2007)

I want my naturalness but not
like I mean it. If I move, the trace
of sorrow shines like some kind
of lie, perhaps the final one
between states of self-restriction.

// Us glittering like our own spark //

Here the night will be nothing,
the origin of everything,
the growth of the final lucid star,
and how the surest way of growth
for us is dying deep in our refusal
to do more than has been done.

Working at Working-class: Lamenting language in the 'poetry' of Aaron Kent
Edna T. Ande, 2019

Aaron Kent has continually made it clear that he is, first and foremost, at the very heart of his being, above all else, a working-class, boot-sale poet, such as in his debut collection *Sleeping with the Frenemy.* The first issue to consider with this declaration is the idea of his self-identity as a poet, but that's something we can save for later inspection. The general concern, here, comes from Kent's identification of himself as working-class. Is there such a thing as the working-class anymore? And if there is, can he, the writer with a BA degree and an MA degree, really be considered working-class?

Kent's primary position in declaring himself working-class comes about from his perception of his use of language as one based and rooted in the deep fundamentals of a working-class dialect, one of accent and indifference to proper, enunciated English. Yes, it is true that there are other factors he has expressed, those of childhood poverty where electricity was too costly for adequate dietary necessities, one of housing and in particular the terraced house he grew up in and the back lane behind it in which he and his friends ran riot, giving his name a bad reputation on the streets he grew up on before the eventual estate move as a teenager, or the hand-me-down nature of materialism he abided by and lived in to help the financial concerns prevalent within the family in which he was raise, all of these expressed in his debut collection *The Kent Boys.* Yet, these are not issues he has evoked or delved into with any depth on a personal level within the rare interviews he gives, or the even rarer readings he has occasionally performed. He has come to terms with these ideas in his poetry, but his social media, and other presence, has been dominated by the working-class tongue.

Glottal stops, basic mispronunciation of 'th' sounds, these aren't signifiers of his working-classness – as if his very core is being at the bottom of a social hierarchy – rather a failure to learn to speak properly.

Clearly, Kent assumes that language is something that is fluid, and open to the whims of a cultural upbringing, and while this can be the case, it certainly isn't with a working-class that has failed to bother with just speaking the goddamn language we were taught. In his, frankly downright derivative poem 'When things get tough [...]' from his debut collection *Houses the Size of Angles*, Kent writes:

> The middle-class won't publish my poems 'cause they don't
> like reality. That and I don't send them poems.

In later poems Kent attempts to cover up his inability to speak properly with apostrophes in place of certain letters, contracting words down to their pseudo-phonetic core. This comes across as laziness, both in his tongue and in his writing, yet also highly indicative of the laziness of the class he belongs to. He uses various similar phrases throughout the debut collection, but lines like 'dose jesters / laffing among the forns' fail to determine one definition or the other of the word 'forns' – Kent mispronouncing thorns as *forns*. Are the jesters laughing among a room full of prickles, of nettles, or are they laughing in the face of baby dear? It is perhaps this failure of his working-class tongue that negatively defines his work, and therefore himself.

Kent has responded to these claims in the past, in his debut collection *Legitimately, I'm Sorry I Suck*, namely stating that taught language is a singular way of attempting to divide a country by social classes, and to ensure that individuals within the country all speak a very white, very upper class English, so others can be determined as just that, the. Kent's belief is that the division of a country into class through means of 'othering the working-class' is a way of ensuring that the majority population determine the lower classes as something to be sneered at and shunned, and this helps to demonise the welfare state and therefore ensure social mobility is null and void. Here, Kent seems to call for an uprising in his poems, demanding the lower class rise up in the friendship the night offers.

Regardless of this, his lack of literary accomplishments, or indeed his lack of thoughts articulated any better than they are in the above poem, does not detract from the fact that Kent is an awful poet who lacks the ability to convey his emotional range in his poetry. His poetry is often stiff and stilted or uses concepts with which he has perhaps only been exposed to in class activism. For example, in the poem 'How could I betray the earth like this' from his debut collection *Breakfast for the Neighbours*, Kent uses the tired trope of mixing up Earth and earth in the title to convey the vague message that he has been made to feel unwelcome in nature and through society, which not only fails to fully express his own emotional journey, but fails to accurately represent experiences of class as transient states.

Like any working-class person with a lack of literary aspirations, Kent has moved through life building friendships with other working-class people, and forming networks of queer ones too, but he also needs to learn how to reach out to those who, unlike him, have been born with a map of emotional trajectories and are able to find their way in a world that is designed to accommodate them. His alienation of the middle-classes reeks of jealousy and resentment and it makes for a pretty depressing read. His smug antagonism and his analysis of the class hierarchy in Britain is effectively cartoonishly simplistic. To the people of the middle-classes, it is as if Kent has decided to pick a side in a fight that they have not even started, as he explains that the working-class 'are figh'n' on diff'r'nt sides'. 'No wonder the class war is hell', reads the final line of this poem.

To put it mildly, Aaron Kent is fatuous, self-indulgent, and frustrating. The desire for an elevated existence and the rejection of the people who can give that to him muddles Kent's personality, rendering it not entirely distinct from its many uncultured detractors. While it is admirable that he wanted to speak out about his experience of not being able to find his place in a classist, heteronormative society, in the end, this fear of not being able to communicate properly ultimately exposes Kent for what he really is; a self-involved, detached moron who should be ashamed of himself rather than given a platform to dispense a universal message of wretchedness that is couched in political terms that don't begin to explain the reality of his life.

Disingenuous Love
(Kent, *The Planet's Radius*, 2017)

We have let time waste away
in shallow increments;
why should we bother performing renditions
of the heron landing hollow
on the flesh and bones of morning
when we could Eat Me gracefully.
There are as many compositions
of life as there are infinite
universes in which
to provide the backing tracks
(and those are only possible that I am).
If we are to be blessed by endemic luck
then I should like to be shoved into the earth,
face first, skull to rust bones
so our children may face the morning,
heron-strong and feral,
imbued by the sacrifice of their father's will
to return to the womb
and to grow to die
and come back to them.

Evidently Trash
(Kent, *The Planet's Radius*, 2017)

There's		the father
	and	the son.
		The water bearer
	and	the small infant.

They	point	to the sky.
They	sing	their song
		to us.

But	no one	says anything.
For	even if	the skies
		have changed,
there	is no more	song
		in them.

That's the Last Time I Watch Performance Art Live
(Kent, *The Planet's Radius*, 2017)

I choose magic, but it doesn't fall;
the notion was as quiet as I was.
Take a flesh tea and squeeze:
competition, work,
get-up, jump, play.

The paranormal is a sensitive platform
where the sunshine is stable.
Now he has won three tinderboxes.
Half-life:
the chimera's adders
appear on the marathon
and flower slowly.

If you ask five cats; cookies are
not a good serviette.
Some do it because I doodle.
Paperboy war with pantheon elements
after the gradual chant of rhododendron:
PANTHEON!

Like snow; have questions:
Notebook! Yes! Etc!
After two minefields,
if confused with a mortician
I will be normal.

Every deadbeat workhouse
avoided a wavelength of persimmon thunder.
Suppose you are against H20
and want to survive several breaches.

Louder and More Menacing
(Kent, *Port Talbot Parkway Train Station Toilets*, 2022)

I am not like your dead body,
how you could die so many times
and still warrant funeral rites.
No, I am stringent and foolhardy,

I am more careful, more deliberate.
You don't have a chance at ordinary grief;
a dog on its back, on its last breath.
Your lips pale and silent embers in your eyes,

a swollen corpus christi; a toothless trunk
in solemnity. I cannot weep, I am the product
of your choosing, the drink you have
and the drink you lost, I am a remedy for thirst.

I am the son of a godless land,
and the father of a landless god.

An Absolute Banger of a Poem
(Kent, *Port Talbot Parkway Train Station Toilets*, 2022)

Long before I believed in bowel complaints,
Perry and I were kids foraging for ants,
he was convinced they taste like strawberries;
something in the acid. He was wrong,
but desperate times and all that;
the cost of living crisis ain't gonna eat itself.

I can't control the weather, but I can definitely control how
long I give myself before I outlive myself (you pipsqueak). Life
is not a honeymoon, never was, merely a guilt trip dressed up
as debt. If the lyric is our best hope at sharing what it means
to be alive, then a whole lot of people really believe 'alive' is
a synonym for family money, a mate at The Guardian, and
a poem about the intricacies of the battle of Agincourt. Not
gonna lie, I had to Google Agincourt,

but I don't need search engines to tell you
how to throw pasty crust at knockers,
or how to bathe two deep in a flower bed.
Every poem has its universe like every month
has its ides, if you beware them all
you can pass go with a healthy dose of scepticism.

When Perry hit his mid-twenties he got married and divorced
within a week, I guess once you believe in the culinary power
of an ant then everything is worth a brief gamble. I've quit
trying to eat my weight in insects, I no longer need to prove
myself.

I've returned as my own Lazarus, Perry,
and now everything is tart as a strawberry.
The best tricks are worth the reveal,
the best resurrections are worth the insatiable desire
for brains. Occasionally, it's worth
putting the method before the mantra.

Continual Concern with Oneself in Aaron Kent's Poetry
Ammé Yedenik, 2019

IT IS NOT always an easy transition to attempt poetry when a writer has found themselves on the outside of literary society – away from Oxbridge and the middle-class, instead slumming it in Redruth. A poem needs a snapshot elucidated past the point of recognition, and then repackaged as an excuse (Bibbard, 2004). How do you glorify the universal when you've spent your whole life forced to focus on the small things, like food and shelter?

There is a line in Aaron Kent's 'Disingenuous Love', from his debut collection *The Planet's Radius*, in which he attempts to create a metaphor for the sacrifice of himself for the growth of his children.

This is unusual for a multitude of reasons, not least that Kent has previously criticised lazy metaphors for sacrifice, calling them both 'inane' and 'narcissistic' in his debut collection *Doomed to Mudlark for Eternity*, so why use it in his poetry? The core theory was that Kent had attempted to showcase how pointless he felt and therefore how inessential his sacrifice for anything would be, though since having children he has grown out of this criticism, proving how weak-willed his personal ideology is. Contemporary poetry criticism, such as that from Bernadette Borisov and Graham Huntere, suggest that Kent has extrapolated the very core of spirituality into his work and found lack (Borisov, 2018), that the only way for him to exist as part of the premise of family is to not be bound by his own flesh, and instead return to the earth, where the burdens of his life are not imposed (Huntere, 2018). Borisov, in particular, asserts that this idea becomes fully formed in the final two lines.

Borisov explains that Kent has returned to a state of non-existence, that he has removed himself from the nuclear family, which was built upon a false premise, and has started to create a family in which diversity and difference is imposed, where every member no longer has to be part of an ideal, and instead can be themselves (Borisov, 2018). She states, with zeal, that Kent's constellations are never confirmed or denied, that they could still be there but he has no longer let them dictate his life, though is still curious enough to look. Borisov believes Kent wants his family to look at the star signs and see them in other people, like caged animals in a zoo, and wonder how they let themselves be so easily perceived.

Upon further inspection, none of the theories hold any water (pun intended) and are instead just the structure of a man grabbing at random strings of words and hoping they form something coherent. Kent writes 'water bearers', implying that there are more than one, which is a strange choice as he is the only Aquarius in his family, and then he proceeds to suggest that these Aquarians may be Leo or Cancer, yet neither of these signs sit either side of his. This coupled with Kent's suggestions that the water bearers 'aren't sure', and that the family 'think' there are constellations, showcase his inability to fully cling to an idea. Earlier in the poem Kent tries to compare an argument with his family in a small space to nuclear destruction. You can almost picture him sat at his desk, smirking proudly at the double meaning of fallout as both an argument and a nuclear incident. He then connects this later with the nuclear family, really hammering the point home, but not entirely making any point clear. Are they a nuclear family because they fight? Did an atom bomb blow up the stars? Is he aware this isn't how bombs work? Why are we taking a detour into star signs? These are all irrelevant ideas tied together by the most fragile of connections – the word 'nuclear.' He then tries to tie the whole theme together with the line 'We strain our necks to look' which is a lovely sentiment, and one in which you can imagine the togetherness of the family as they stare into the void and try to wonder where they fit in. This is a delicate moment. Unfortunately, it is all the more delicate for its rarity.

The mawkishness is visible in the next two poems in the collection, 'Evidently Trash' and 'That's the Last Time I Watch Performance Art Live'. This feels like a break in the inter-family intimacy Kent discusses and a slight shift away from the particular. The caged animals, the plutonium, these are all symbolic touches used to hit the big issues, but with a very thin hint of the foundations for understanding a functioning family and the relationship that bonds them. The idea of raising a family together is relevant but Kent seems to know it's not. He talks about 'persimmon thunder' in the sky and of his family looking into the distant light, but does not elaborate on how they are looking for constellations, when they are already in them (in the 'fractal version' of the constellations). This inability to produce anything vaguely interesting outside of his own selfishness is a real shame, but these poems are too thin, and too unconvincing, to warrant an entire essay exploring their every twist and turn.

The final impression left by Kent is of an individual that is unable to hold himself and the family together. His negativity about life is reflected in the lack of ambition he has to make himself seem interesting or funny. This is compounded by the laziness of his language. It is a song of longing, but only a song of longing for himself. Kent's life is perhaps best summed up by some words of his own from his debut collection *Port Talbot Parkway Train Station Toilets*, 'I am the son of a Godless land / and the father of a landless God.'

The Treaty You Couldn't Write
(Kent, *Some Bullshit about Rabbit*s, 2019)

and so they all sprawl before us.
      They are absurd. Exhausted
of everything that can be said.
      They have nothing to say to us and
the echoes of that grave bed
      of our past, over of life, shows
the width of its defiance. But there
      is also something. The idea was not
        invented by us. A human

stamped on every parent and child, every school,
      every epic. It is the same. It is bigger than life.
And why should it be true? It is true
      because it is our private illusion,
it is the most splendid lily.
      Our foolery is the source
of what has stood us still through generations.
      Neither the profligate glow of Dionysus's power,
        nor the wildfire banqueting

of Poseidon, neither the desperate charisma
      of Eros, nor the relentless aggression
of Ares- He alone knows the cost
      of this love: each can kill or be killed.
And we have lived on grains of cloud as so many
      living birds of the morning have
        dared to bend and hold a branch, strike down

by the merciless allure of the glass-
      eyed eye which flicks the tongue
and makes you suffer. But still we hold

our feathers until the last bird flies,
and it may be that we win, and leave
        in some obscure fire a fluttering handful
            of hair. But what if we lose?

But When is the Last Bird
(Kent, *Some Bullshit about Rabbits*, 2019)

We have lived on the
slightest breath of our own
that the last will never
be as brief as the last breath
we have lost in the night.
The idea is an old one. The notion
of the human soul, of its capacity
to carry all creation inside it: the idea
has its origin in the myth we are
all creatures. We have been told:
There was a time when we were happy
and sang of it and lived in it
and named the time before them
and the time after them,
and when it was over
we forgot the time of happiness.
But what if the words
do not fall out of my mouth?
I am talking a language
They cannot understand.
In the long ago they took away
a hundred eyes to see all the world in.
I am singing the names of
those that wept the tears.
What if the song does
not fall from my lips?

No one I know of has seen the whole world in a year
(Kent, *Nature Poetry as a Prize Plea*, 2020)

We have lived on dreams
like the Cosmic Owl has
driven us through the universe
and given us voices of the dead.

We saw them grow up
out of the corner of our eyes
and then a great hand
came upon us. We slept.

What if we were dreaming?
What if they were still
no bigger than milk and
every rash a doctor's visit?

We have heard their voices,
voices of undeniable truth,
and they whisper: We're sorry,
there's no such thing as dreams.

Efflorescence

(Kent, *Nature Poetry as a Prize Plea*, 2020)

If I made music, that'd be one thing,
but my soul is a cat curled up in darkness,
my heart a saxophone fallen under the ocean.
I have never told anyone why I'm drawn
to those parts, why they make me cry,
but I know I am clawing myself back.
There's a way to make a sound
and keep the music inside myself.
I want to die with my lungs aching to be a bird,
I want the bones of me to sing.
I will find, in my skin, the secret of a door
and the universe inside of the rooms of me.
Help, I think I'm trapped inside of a fire-fly.

First Nightmare at 5
(Kent, *Catatonic Rehearsal*, 2022)

The rendered sphere effervescent along
Mercury's retrograde, serendipitous
cusp markers for circumstance.

We move entrenched in weakness
by cosmic winged guardians of
intravenous nightmare O drip-fed.

Life as interminable disturbance
metered out in seismic splendour,
the children waking from dread.

Interview with Aaron Kent
The Duck Egg Review

Interviewer:
R P JHYNNE
ONLINE EXCLUSIVE
July 2019

Q To what extent do you consider yourself to be a working-class poet?

A I mean, to what extent do you consider yourself a middle-class journalist? It depends, I guess, on how much you define yourself by your class. Am I a working-class teacher? Am I a working-class father? Am I a working-class pedestrian when I walk down the street? I think 'probably' is the answer to those questions, but I don't think that works for other classes. The working-class, from my perspective, are continually defined in negative terms, as if to remind people that they are in fact the other, the thing to avoid. It's easier not to define yourself as working-class because it can shut a lot of doors and open a lot of stereotypes. Which is why I decided to go for it, to define myself before someone else defines me.

Q That sounds like nonsense, like you're reaching. Surely either everybody is defined by their class or everybody isn't?

A I doubt you've been turned down from a job because of the way you speak, or because you don't have that academic look, or because you don't have those good connections the upper-classes do. Experience is key to failure when you're working-class; actually growing up in a crappy terraced house – with a roof insulated with beer bottles and newspapers, with doorbell wire used to wire up the whole house, that ain't gonna (sp) get me anywhere. But some poet with famous parents, and that good money, who talks street, who talks about a struggle they didn't have, they can appropriate my culture and succeed. A lot of publishers don't actually want you to be working-class. They just want the story, not the person.

Q Who are these mythical poets you talk about? It seems you just can't accept that you aren't as well received as you'd like, and you're using your class as a defence.

A Well, I'm not going to name names, I'm not that person, and I'm sure people will have their own opinions on it. The idea that my class is a defence mechanism against a lack of reception is bizarre, I wasn't well received or read when I wasn't writing about class, like my debut book *Some Bullshit about Rabbits* (2019), or my debut book *Nature Poetry as a Prize Plea* (2020), some new book ain't gonna (sp) change that. But, I do think it's harder for the working-class to break through. Using working-class language and tropes after you went to Oxbridge and are best mates with big name editors is a sure fire route to success, but actually being that person, and not having that route or those connections doesn't get you anywhere fast.

Q Here's the thing, there are working-class poets who went to Oxbridge and don't speak wrong–

A There it is, don't speak 'wrong'. My voice ain't (sp) wrong. And you can stop with the '(sp)'s – you have been brought up to believe there is a right and wrong way to talk, and anything outside of white, middle/upper class is wrong, but that ain't the case. Curriculums are designed to tell us how to be and how to grow up, but those curriculums are designed through a very narrow scope and a very specific culture. There are so many people who don't fit into that scope and don't want to fit into it – but they're being forced to, because that's what we're told. I've read about politicians who were taught to speak like the working-class to appeal to us, they're using our voice to kill us. I mean, people have derided me for eating with a fork in my right hand and knife in my left, but the correct side on which to hold cutlery is just some idea some pleb passed down as tradition, like there's no basis in it as a universal truth.

Q But Aaron, you wrote this interview, you conducted it with yourself for your book – even the interviewer's name is a lazy spoonerism of J H Prynne – an influence of yours.[2]

A Of course I did, I made up the Paris Review-type interview too, there's no way a publication like that interviews people like me. I don't mean that in a spiteful, nasty way, it's just there's people all over the place who are like me and who have a voice, we all talk the same language, but we aren't recognised because we are working-class, we aren't recognised because we have different ways of looking, our voice isn't understood. I've been told my voice is working-class, or sometimes just told I sound common. I don't think they want the common person in their literary spaces.

Q You don't consider yourself a poet?

A I consider myself a working-class writer. The working-

---

[2] I've had several people assume that Prynne is my biggest influence, and while he has influenced my work, he isn't the biggest influence. I think the most interesting creative work is one where disparate influences are held in equal measure, rather than acting as a platform for the artist to imitate the work they admire. Work that is influenced equally by Keith Buckley, JH Prynne, and Tracy Emin, while creating art that feels indebted to neither of the three, for example, would interest me a lot more than work that is a mere imitation of the artist's favourite person.

class person and the middle-class person may speak the same language, in other words they may use the same tropes, but the way that their language is read is different. Just because you speak the same language don't mean you speak the same voice.

Q You're being a complete dick.

A How come you're being such a good guy then?

Q Because this is an interview. I am hired to be more professional and articulate than the kind of language you're using. I asked you what you want to say here, and you're not being honest.

A And you're speaking to me as a middle-class person.

Q But you haven't been honest. You say you're working-class and there's this invisible middle-class enemy – but maybe it's just that you're the problem, not everybody else.

A I don't give a fuck, you can take my interview and do what you like with it.

Q I can do the same I did with your debut, Catatonic Rehearsal (2022). I saw it at a fellow writer's house and burnt it while he was out of the room.[3]

A Cool story.

Q Thanks.

---

[3] This is a true story in which I know a poet who found a very limited copy of their debut collection, which they hated, at another poet's house. When the poet/homeowner left the room, the poet/guest burnt the book.

Screenshot of Waking
(Kent, *Feels like a Bloody Fairytale,* 2012)

Eclipse the midnight
with your difficult rhythms, sleep,
amalgamate a phantasmagoric ebb
and flow into fever's rough edges
with growing notes of disturbed crises.

Stretch dayglo insomnia across
the vast loneliness of the hands
upon which it advocates.

Spread yourself thin across
a windscreen as resolution
to a still life of sleep.

Cataclysm, Thy Name is Aaron
(Kent, *Abject Permanence*, 1999)

We wielded ourselves
to the caskets of sunflower
seeds, split succulent, burnt
back like a dead man's hairline.
In atrophy we clamoured
for reasons to love gentle
interruptions, to hold diametric
ends of measurement in swaddling cloth.

> You know what I mean when I say
> I'm scared of the reason I am what I said
> I'd be. When I am my reason for my anger at
> my own insistence. I, that I embody,
> caught in my dismal architecture.
> My own nature my reason to find fault
> in all I have offered and all I gave to
> my own definitive clause to hate me, unbidden.

We soften awake across the shadow
of Jupiter's closest passing.
A family of astronauts reacting
to minute galactic progression.
There is no time to render
nightmares into prose, morning
has begged us awake
for the school run.

When you Wake you'll Believe you are a Theatre Critic
(Kent, *The One and Only Tony Lonely*, 2017)

(I)
Concentricity is measured in vaudeville
performers weighing down on an imitation
of intimacy. It isn't, but stick a line
like that in a poem and you've subverted
any expectation the reader had.

(II)
A transmission is what happens
when status is blind to
somebody else's energy,
and here I am held hostage
to every phantasmagorical museum
I've constructed on a wave of insomnia.

(III)
I don't know all the science, sure,
but would I like to be a scientist?
No, though I'd do anything for eight
or so millimetres of mercury.

(IV)
If I could eat my weight in money
I'd waste a perfectly valuable
financial investment but at least
I'd get the taste of how much
I loathe myself: humid August drug-
sticky, sweet like liquorice I imagine.

Synonyms for Inheritance
(Kent, *The Universe Won't Remember Us*, 2020)

I'm again we're moving sorry,
eye nerve for the feels when
my pupils itch; the squelch
lets me alive to know and good to
make the hand move the music follow.

Instrument the silence perceptible
as movement away from four four.
Two four than four more, too far
from Thor for thunder to worry be-
and-love like ridden two years.

I scratch into headaches my skin,
can't riches my share then arrive
as words in political din. In the finest
sense, near the people of the deep
calling estate for renewed revelation.

Guess What? I Hate Thatcher
(Kent, *Facial Recall*, 2017)

The news says
she was a great
woman, they bullshit
her as a visionary,
a leader, a force
to be reckoned with,
and I, a working-class
scumbag, live with the
wreckage of her hate.

Review of Aaron Kent's The Working Classic
Reviewed by Dane G. Brunt

Some may disagree, but good confessional poetry comes from a place of bringing your truest self to the page – as much as one can showcase 'truth' on a page, I mean, what gets left out, what is and isn't truth, whose truth is relevant: the poets? The reader? These are questions not necessary here, because Kent has intended to bring himself to the page, and instead brought a real shame.

We get it, we get it from the title page, we get it from the first line of the first damn poem – Kent is working-class scum. This attempt to define himself does not come across as punk, or rebellious, it comes across as self-pitying and lazy. The main fault of this debut book comes from Kent's determination to consistently berate us, the reader, with his belief that the working-class are treated as the scourge of the society, only for him to present poems that demonstrate his scummy upbringing.

He can't sleep now, and couldn't sleep as a kid in his poem 'Screenshot of Waking', the description of his insomnia as 'dayglo' representing the garishness of his medical conditions also being common, chavvy, cringey. He hates himself for bringing children into a world that sucks in 'Cataclysm, Thy Name is Aaron' (an absolutely abysmal attempt at a title). He is torn between saving money and eating it in 'When you Wake you'll Believe you are a Theatre Critic'. A childhood friend of his died in 'The Reservoir', and low socio-economic status people are plotting rebellion in 'Synonyms for Inheritance'. And he hates Thatcher, like continually hates Thatcher in several pieces including the nail on head poem that is 'Guess What? I Hate Thatcher'. All of this is Kent telling us how much the working-class is kept underfoot, but none of it is poetry – rather just brute force storytelling.

Perhaps most unforgivably, Kent doesn't know, or want, to follow the rules of grammar and punctuation, some poems forgo capitals, others apostrophes, some don't even follow basic English as he attempts to recreate his voice on the page. It feels scatty, and underdeveloped, and lazy.

Kent is not an interesting poet, this is evident from his debut pamphlet *Facial Recall*, and his debut collection *Unfolding Rue*, but he has pushed it to the limits of boredom here. Poem after poem about how common he is, line after line about his poor family life, stanza after stanza about his goddamn accent. Kent would do well to remember that there are other working-class writers out there, and maybe if they all just accepted that with a bit of work, a determination to learn to speak the proper tongue, and maybe less moaning they might get somewhere.

It pains me to say this, but as Aaron's father, I can't help but feel disappointed in his work. As a parent, I want nothing more than to tell him how proud I am of him, how much I love him and how much I believe in him. But I just can't seem to find the words to express these feelings to him, and it breaks my heart.

I can see how much Aaron has struggled with his working-class identity and the challenges that come with it. But instead of using his experiences to create poetry that resonates with people on a deeper level, he has fallen into the trap of self-pity and victimhood. His poetry lacks the nuance and subtlety that make good poetry truly impactful, and instead relies on tired themes and repetitive storytelling.

Furthermore, I can't help but feel frustrated by his disregard for basic rules of grammar and punctuation. It's as if he's not even trying to put in the effort to make his poetry the best it can be. I know he has a unique voice and perspective, but it feels like he's not doing justice to his talent.

I hope that Aaron can find a way to channel his

experiences into poetry that truly captures the complexity and beauty of the human experience. As his father, I want nothing more than to see him succeed and be happy, and I know that he has the potential to do great things if he just puts in the effort. But for now, I can't help but feel disappointed in this collection and hope that he can learn from his mistakes and grow as a poet.

I do love you, Aaron, and I am proud of you. I told you that before your mother and I left when we visited over Christmas, remember? We phoned to tell you we'd made it safely to the motorway, and you said 'I love you both', to which your mum replied 'I love you too', and I said it too. I've worried, ever since that day, that you didn't hear me – I know you said you heard it, you told your mother you did when she asked, but did you really? I hope so, Aaron, I really do.[4]

I'm sorry for the bad review. I love you.

---

[4] I didn't hear it. I told him that I did, but the phone had already hung up.

A Poem So Meta Mark Zuckerberg Filed a Lawsuit
(Kent, *Manic State*, 2020)

Oceanic as a metaphor opening a hatch
some 200 odd metres below sea level.
> *I'll be honest, I've never learnt to tie shoelaces,*
> *I get by with luck and some nifty sleight of hand.*
I used to dream of coffins, now I sleep calcifying
diary entries into a convenient arrangement of stanzas.
If I cared about reality, I'd consider describing
my coldsore, my hayfever, my propensity
for believing in my own eventual suicide.
I think my brain is bleeding again,
but it's too early to tell; it'll be less strawberry
more the colour of a truck reversing.
I've begun cutting eyes in bedsheets cause
I'm desperate for your return, I've heard
ghosts smell like yesterday's rainfall
but everybody I've lost smelt of Mad Dog 2020.
Yeah, I concede, this doesn't live up
to the strength of its own billing,
still, it's taken me 8 weeks to write.

How I am the smallest thing at the largest times possible
(Kent, *Manic State*, 2020)

Let the brilliant ones in,
the strange sacred ones, the scary ones,
the brave ones, let them shine
against the sun-glazed stars.
Let us make angels
and kiss their cosmic cheeks.
I've got a little list
of all the colours & scents & sounds
in this ocean of space.

All along it seems we're waiting
for a different weather
I want no more for us
than an ordinary life of ordinary days
This is just my bones shaking,
there's no heart left in me
(but) I'd prefer ghosts
& their hands
& their fingers tapping
inside the veins of the radiators.

You turn to me, *stop all your dreaming,*
let us finally rest
in one another's arms.
and let me tell you a story.

We are the same flesh of the same dead man
(Kent, *Manic State*, 2020)

I haven't written in so long,
but I would start by writing
about yams if I knew
what yams were.

I was scared of something
as I began this,
but I have forgotten what it was;
if I end up overdrawn
or cowering in a Costa Coffee
know there is something wrong -
I'm a Nero guy.

I'll endeavour to smile
when the world explodes,
or I'll be sad. I won't actually
know until it happens
and then it'll be too late:
chunks of us all
seasoning a primordial soup
of sweet potatoes.

Glorified Gym Etiquette
(Kent, *Manic State*, 2020)

Those men are fucking
in the gym again, the owner
has asked then to stop
or at least wipe their fresh
love from the machines
so other men can fuck
on the treadmill after.

Those men are fucking
again, using free weights
as new states of euphoria,
pummelling jackhammer
in the mirrors so they can
watch their sheen as gloss.

One day the men will have
to stop fucking in the gym
and actually do some reps,
until then as long as the machines
are clean and their grunts
don't crack open the shell of
our secrets, I think we're fine.

a fine harvest
(Kent, *Manic State*, 2020)

Ah! You'll break my nose
with that smile.
All of those good lovers,
we're going to miss them,
maybe they'll be back
in some rainbow vision
after the sun's gone.

My insides are shaped like a road,
although it may be solipsistic –
here's to the endless cycle
of hypochondria & sermons.
I used to think of my lungs like fish
gasping outwards over the fizz
of fresh coldsores, now
I'm ashamed of that.
There's no heart in me
just blood pushing my body
around in its grave.

BBC RADIO POETICS
Interview with Discovery Jones

DISCOVERY JONES
You've firmly established yourself as an artist.

AARON KENT
That's where I want to be, I want to be the artist, I want to be the artist who gives you the gift, not the artist that keeps your gift the rest of the time. I'm making the most beautiful gifts I've ever made. I'm creating new visions, I'm creating new things, I'm making the best art I've ever made. And I'm going to give you the gift. I'm going to give you the gift. I'm going to give you the gift of being a human being. I'm going to give you the gift of a vision, a true vision, I'm going to give you the gift of a new world, a new paradigm. I'm going to give you that gift, and that's where I want to be and I want to go, I want to go to bed at night and wake up the next day not saying today I have got to get on a plane and I have got to do something with these words. Like this art is so powerful that when I do have a problem I am not going to let that problem – I want to say that I don't have a problem, I'm going to say that I'm at peace. I'm at peace. I'm at peace with myself, I am at peace with my fans, I am at peace with my life, I am at peace with the people who are on tour. If I have a problem it's going to be about who I have to fight with, but I'm at peace. I'm at peace with all of them because they can't tell the difference. They don't know what to say. They can't even talk.

DISCOVERY JONES
You've been open in the past about your BPD, about these moments of mania where you write reams of work over days, and then spend weeks destroying everything you've written and hating it all.

AARON KENT

Because sometimes I can't do the things I'm meant to do, and I have no other way to express it. I don't know.

DISCOVERY JONES

So I was wondering if you've had an experience like that in the last year.

AARON KENT

I have to write new beginnings. I have to start again. I have to start again. The beginning is a part of me and I need to find a way to work with that in my poetry, and all the other things, the writing, the living, the dying. Always the dying. Always. I was born dying. How does that sound? How does that sound?

DISCOVERY JONES
You were born dying?

AARON KENT

I have to do what I have to do, I know it. I know it. But poetry is the thing I love the most because it's my nature to do this, and I love it and I want to keep doing it. This is why I have these new names, these new voices. I have to be reborn, I have to go and put the fire back in me, put the spirit back in me.

DISCOVERY JONES
What about what you wrote before?

AARON KENT

I will never allow any of it. I will never allow it. My only salvation is in my art, that's all. If my life has to suffer, the life I live – the life I live – my life is my art, and my art is my life. I'm all over the place. I'm all over the place. I'm all over the place.

You're all over the place. The art is the life, it's my life. What is it that we know? Is it not that something is the most important thing in our lives that is of value to us? If we live life, we know that art is our most valuable thing. What I know for sure is the most important thing I know for sure is that we are born to die and I don't want to be born to die, I want to be born to live. I want to live to give life to the people who are alive, to the people who are going to be born. It's my life, I have to do that. It's my life, and it's my death, and I want to live and I want to live to give life. It's going to take me twenty-four hours to put on my make-up, or six weeks, I don't know, maybe a year to get into the right frame of mind and be able to go out there and say it again.

DISCOVERY JONES
I've been working with an artist and they wanted to ask you about your moments of madness, because they were wondering about whether a moment of madness is just like an act of God, or whether they might be able to use it.

AARON KENT
That's the most dangerous question, I love it! That's the most dangerous question, because what is art? What is art? I'm going to say everything is art. I'm going to say everything is art. Like, people will allude to the fact that this whole book is a sort of monologue between myself and myself, so it's all an act of creation, but it's taken me 5 years, and there is truth in it – the BPD, the mania is true. I can't sleep. I rarely sleep. I stay up and I write, and I overload until I just hate myself and want to die, then I want the music of life, then I want the solemnity of death. Everything is a fucking joke if you choose to laugh. And everything is a fucking act of god if you choose to die, if you choose to stop the show, I don't know what I choose, but at least I get to choose what I choose. That's what I choose.

DISCOVERY JONES
So how could a moment of madness have a life like that?

AARON KENT
If the moment of madness is an act of God – and an act of God is an act of God, if the act of God is an act of God – then I can only choose to live in the life and create the art that I'm creating because everything in art that is created by me is a piece of me, and I'm living life, that's it. And everything in life that I create for myself is part of my art, and I'm creating the art that I love. All I can say, as the artist that I am, I'm going to create art, even though it's going to be fucking ugly. I'm going to create art, I'm going to create an act of God. I'm going to act out what I'm feeling at that moment because it will be the only way I can express myself. I can't live. I can't die. I'm trying to find a way to do both, I'm trying to find a way to do both. I want to live, and I want to die. I'm still in the process of finding a way to do both. And I'm not done with that either.

DISCOVERY JONES
I didn't realise you believed in a God?

AARON KENT
I do and I don't. Actually, I just don't care if there is or isn't a God. I don't care. I know He's there and I know He's not there. I don't care. I don't care. The same way you know there's the sun and there's the moon and you don't care. You don't care.

DISCOVERY JONES
I've found that the more I've believed in the sun, the more I've believed in the moon, the more I've wondered if there's something else.

AARON KENT

I see what you mean, but this is my art, so when I look at the moon or the sun it's part of my art. The same way you look at the shadow of the tree and the face of a man, and the moon is the character, or you look at a perfect blue sky and the meaning of life is told by this dog or the sky is telling you something, whatever it is, or the sky is telling you something. It's my interpretation of it. I created it, I'm the artist, and I'm not going to take it down because I believe in a God. That's bullshit. If I believed in a God, I'd be on my knees in the street begging for forgiveness every day of my life.

DISCOVERY JONES

So are you a nihilist?

AARON KENT

No.

DISCOVERY JONES

It seems like you're saying that everything is an act of creation, that everything is art.

AARON KENT

Yes, exactly. Everything is art. Life is art, death is art, madness is art. It's all art, and it's all beautiful. And that's what I'm trying to capture in my work. I want to capture the beauty of life, the beauty of death, the beauty of madness. I want to create something that's never been done before, something that's truly unique and special.

DISCOVERY JONES

Nihilist, I don't know why I used that word, I hate it.

AARON KENT
Yeesh, looking back, I was really wild during this interview.

DISCOVERY JONES
This interview now?

AARON KENT
Yeah, this was peak BPD me. Us.

Superparamagnets

(Kent, *Definitive Reasons to Drown*, 2022)

This tangible projection of violence
has its compound within a waltz

of fists before learning to dance.
We have operated alongside

harbour's paraffin crew, ingested
emulsion's stubborn repair.

A bolus of us screened for daylight,
for our desire to bite into human flesh.

Each of us a render for the myth
of palms forcing nasal cavity into matter

upwards as a bullet between space
arranged to cushion a brain, to manifest

grief as a tangible marker eroding
optic nerves enacting their own violence.

Recommendations Upon Seeing a Ghost
(Kent, *Definitive Reasons to Drown*, 2022)

Ask them for a name.
    The name they give
    may not necessarily be yours.

If the ghosts are tight
    with money it may indicate
    an ulcer is forthcoming.

Offer to end the world
    as revenge for whatever
    tragedy they're haunting.

Remember they're here
    For a memory, not you.
    Memories can't eat.

Whisp about on the cusp
    of some hand-me-down
    from a time before period dramas.

It's only a seance
    if you promise not to send
    otherworldly dick pics.

Remain calm and composed
    in the face of
    a slaughtered pig.

Deliver yourself to their
    paper thin presence, all chronic
    illness and murder victim.

Allow them to feel for the crevices
        of your brain's failure
        to deliver you home to them.

Insomnia's Shop-worn Presence
(Kent, *A Guide to Necessary Resuscitation*, 2024)

Given the choice, I would
be an upcycled feather
of some flightless bird,
gold hue, fine painted
pheasant as riposte to
a catacomb of night,
of reverting to myself
as a toddler, all glazed
eyes and stolen childhood.

Historically I've been
scared of my own
shadow when I see it
puppeteering knives,
an auditorium of gentle
violence beset by venom
as a valentine's card.
In eating myself for
breakfast I am saving
us from a weakness
that registers its own
delicious intrusive thoughts.

The sound of blisters,
the smell of dirt, and now
the choice of guts
to stuff ourselves with,
to stoke when the flies come,
so they go. Five fresh livers
laid out by a skinny man.
I have no eyes. I can not

look upon the taste of bile
burning a scream to the stars,
we were once that free.

Upon considering the jump
(Kent, *A Guide to Necessary Resuscitation*, 2024)

my mother tells me to leave
behind a small hydra,
it could loop itself into
a nine-to-five, she suggests.
We are undermined by sheet
lightning and the glare of a laser
pen flicking about for eyes,
an infrared forked tongue.

But the school day runs half
eight to four, and my propensity
for becoming a small gelatinous
sphere needs no understudy.
A sessile child sees suicide
as success, I whisper, and
biological immortality cares
not for a prostrate body.

My brother shits the bed,
my father cooks hot dogs
in a toaster, and I attempt
to capture thunderclaps with
a red diode beam. On the flight
home I come to understand
a good magician puts the
spectacle ahead of the warning.

I'm the Shit and I'm Knee Deep in it
(Kent, *A Guide to Necessary Resuscitation*, 2024)

I'm working on this backwards walk counting stars and
both those moons.

I'm working on these moods and this mourning and all
these stops and starts are chaos.

I've been working on my walking wrong at breakneck
speeds forth into fords.

I've been working on my blindness and my blindness and
my brain.

I'm working on intrusive thoughts and the drugs and the
crying and the shame.

I'm working on these zero-point dreams that tell me all
hands are barometers.

I've been working on small time-sensitive shifts from central
to peripheral to centre.

I've been working on the ocean and the wind and a way to
haunt colours.

I'm working on widening ways my end can be called a
revelation.

I'm working on a complex sigh four seconds before I hit the
ground.

I'm working on real contact highs and I'm working on falling apart.

I'm working on gathering up all of my loose change.

Aaron Kant Keep Living: An interview with the poet
Conducted by: Henly Imostok

Aaron Kent is an easy figure to miss, which is an odd thing to say about a broad-shouldered, bearded, 6 foot 2 guy, but he does all he can to make himself fade into the backdrop – his posture is poor, his clothes are dull and poorly fitted and he has a habit of averting his eyes when you talk to him. He's not a bad looking guy, but he doesn't have the charisma to stand out. Ironically, this is how it feels to read his poetry; it's not bad, but it doesn't have enough to stand out. 'Maybe that's unfair,' I suggest upon first meeting him, 'maybe I just don't care for all the self-hatred?' Kent shrugs, 'maybe.'

Kent's poetry is a reflection of himself; it's full of low self-esteem, insecurity and fear. It's a reflection of his inability to stand out, his inability to have an opinion or make a decision. His poetry is like a lovesick, broken hearted teenager, too self-conscious to make the first move or the first step.

'I'm not sure that's fair,' Kent says, 'but maybe it is.'

I try to prod him on this point, to push him into some sort of an answer beyond the inane posturing of somebody who clearly wishes they were elsewhere. He may not know where that elsewhere is, and I can guarantee he'd be unhappy there too if he found it, but it's obvious that he is mostly uncomfortable with just having to exist.

'I don't know,' he says eventually, 'I just feel like I'm not really worth the effort of whatever it is that manifested me into existence.'

And that's the crux of the matter; Kent isn't a man who doesn't feel like he's doing anything with his life. He's confident in his love for poetry and the written word, and he knows what he is doing in that field, or at least he feels like he does. Kent is, instead, somebody who just doesn't see the point in their own presence, who doesn't understand why they have to toil upon this realm.

'I've written quite often about how little I mean to me,' he tells me, 'and I think there is a belief that I may be writing in that style as a throwback to some emo version of myself, but I'm not miserable and I'm not inherently sad. I guess I don't see the purpose in surviving, and maybe that's because I've had to do a lot of surviving: as a working-class kid, as a rape survivor, as a brain haemorrhage victim - maybe those things just took it out of me and the need to drink a glass of water at midday to keep functioning seems so dull in comparison.'

Kent is not a man who is looking for sympathy or attention. In his recent debut collection of poetry, titled *A Guide to Necessary Resuscitation* he attempts a new style of poetry, something he has tentatively titled Post-Poetry as a nod to genres of music that try to look past the standard style. Here, in these poems, Kent is most interested in trying to be explicit about the inner monologue that interrupts his writing. 'I have these things, these deep self-truths, I stop myself from sharing when writing, so these poems allow those feelings to surface and no longer be hidden or disguised by metaphor.'

I try to push him, to understand why somebody who doesn't see the necessity of survival is so keen to write. 'I guess I just feel like if I'm going to be here, I may as well be honest about it,' he says. 'I don't think I'm looking for a way to escape reality, I'm just attempting honesty in a world that often feels dishonest.'

My favourite poems from his debut collection *Definitive Reasons to Drown* are 'Recommendations upon Seeing a Ghost' and 'Upon considering the jump'. In the former, Kent gives a voice to the long-deceased spectral ancestors looking for somebody to implement the rules of contacting the afterlife. In the latter, he writes of his first moment of suicidal ideation at twelve years old, stood on a balcony, telling his mother he thinks he'd like to kill himself, and in doing so he shows a surprising amount of self-forgiveness and empathy. It's a reminder that, despite everything, Kent is still a human being with feelings and emotions. He may not see the point in his own existence, but he is still capable of caring for others.

'I think that's what it comes down to,' he says, 'I don't see the point in my own survival, but I see the value in other people's. Maybe that's why I write, to try and show other people that they are valuable, that their lives have meaning.'

As I finish up the interview, Kent thanks me for taking the time to speak with him and offers to send me a copy of his latest work. I agree, and we part ways.

But as I leave the coffee shop, I can't shake the feeling that something was off about the whole interaction. Kent's disinterest in his own existence seemed too rehearsed, too calculated. And then it hits me – the way he spoke about his poetry and his writing style, it was almost like he was trying to sell it to me, to convince me of its value.

I quickly pull out my phone and get in touch with my contact, who confirms my suspicions – Aaron Kent is a known spy for The Literary Establishment, a secretive organization dedicated to promoting certain types of literature and poetry.

They recruit struggling writers and poets, promising them fame and success in exchange for pushing their agenda.

It all makes sense now – Kent's self-deprecating attitude was a cover, a way to make himself seem unimportant and unremarkable. His focus on being honest in his writing was a ploy to make his work seem authentic and genuine. And his insistence on the value of other people's lives was a thinly veiled attempt to promote the Literary Establishment's agenda of making him seem like a real class act.

I realize with a sinking feeling that I've been played, that this whole interview was just a way for Kent to promote his work and the work of the Literary Establishment. But I can't help but feel a grudging respect for their tactics – they may be manipulative, but they're also incredibly effective. And as I walk away, I can't help but wonder how many other writers and poets are secretly working for them, promoting their agenda under the guise of creative expression.

The Word that Stands for Nothing
(Kent, *Circadian Rhythm Fashion Week*, UNPUBLISHED)

My dreams have been inescapable
        for the past 2 years.
Sometimes I wake to find my face
        glued to the toilet seat,
and then, when I set off to make coffee
I find my face searing away on the grill
        at a restaurant.

So I can't sleep, it's not a choice.
        I think it might be the Time Lord
who has kept me awake
        with Imodium and a prayer
and I'm going to find him and stab him
in the back with a knife
        made from my own shit.

First Breath Upon Waking
(Kent, *Circadian Rhythm Fashion Week*, UNPUBLISHED)

I watched the birds all day. I had more broken bones than I could count. Every time I stood a broken bone fell from my body. One fell into the grass. One fell into my lap. One fell into the pond, but it didn't stick there. I caught one in my mouth and swallowed it down. It seemed that all of my bones were broken. My feet were broken. My clavicles were broken. The clouds were broken. Nothing was intact. I didn't see anything that wasn't broken. I didn't feel anything that wasn't broken. I didn't know how to feel anything that wasn't broken. The sky wasn't blue. It was more intense than blue. I thought I could feel it, but it was hard to put my hand to something so large. I was afraid to try because I couldn't imagine anything that could feel whole. There was something in my eyes that felt loose, but I wasn't sure how I felt about that. I decided that crying in public was something I would never do. I wasn't sure why I wanted to keep that in mind, but it was true. I liked the truth. I liked that a single bone could make all the difference. I was afraid that if I looked away from the broken bones, the broken bones would still be broken. When I did look away, I thought I saw an unbroken tree. Then I looked back, and it was still broken, and I started to feel bad for the tree. So, I looked away. Then I looked back. The broken tree was still broken. I had no idea what to do about that, so I decided to look away again. But then I couldn't help looking back. And then, the broken tree wasn't the only broken tree anymore.

Excessive Daytime Sleepiness in Stroke Survivors
(Kent, *Circadian Rhythm Fashion Week*, UNPUBLISHED)

It's a vacuum within.
Empty and waiting.

The ragged squalling voices appear
the smell of pine is everywhere.
No noise
no animals.

If there is no sound,
then I see nothing.
I cannot speak.

My words just
remain
black glittering lines
outside of me.

Too bad
that I am not a cartoon.

I would be hilarious.

Frank Skinner's Honeymoon Tour

(Kent, *Circadian Rhythm Fashion Week*, UNPUBLISHED)

The first stop, somewhere south of climate change, is an underwater shipwreck. It should not be there. We have not been there before. The possibilities are endless. Something big is in there, in the dark with a few old men sitting around with umbrella drinks, smoking cigarettes, and shivering. It could be the skeleton of a huge atoll, for all we know. Or it could be a rotting diamond teller, perhaps they had a black hole at their wedding. We have seen each other under these lights so often. This could be a horror movie. All kinds of bizarre things come out of this wreck Just don't point your fingers at the light. You will not like what happens then. Maybe it will grab your finger. Not sure, not for sure, but maybe. It is hard to say. It might. So, on the first stop we may find something remarkable. This could happen and we won't ever be the same again.

Evoking the Corpse of a Celebrity who Faked their Death
(Kent, *Circadian Rhythm Fashion Week*, UNPUBLISHED)

If I kindly exchange enough trauma
I might be able to buy breakfast
for every man here sharing their
diddled by our early leaders. All
of these organisers are animals
with cobwebbed teeth, renumerating
themselves for renumerating our
stories. The first time I died I stopped

dreaming. The second time I died I
stopped understanding where the
dreams end. If I die again rest me
on top of old cairn stones and I'll
revisit in a luminous gas from some
world that isn't ours, one that is
more lucid than boiling water stretched
over the soft matter of a brain.

Funny guy, believing I could write
when all I have is intrusive thoughts
of creating a stand-up routine around
my stroke. When I got out of hospital,

a family member had a small brain
bleed, barely registering like the evocation
of a prayer, or the semblance of a spirit,
the end credits scene of a disaster movie,
every single cinematic superhero,

weakened by doubt and insecurity,
riddled with decrepit bones, ashamed

of a history of violence. If I stand
still and stare into the dark long enough,
I can see us spin away from the stars.

Like the Broken Sunlight or a Wooden Door
(Kent, *Circadian Rhythm Fashion Week*, UNPUBLISHED)

Oh, good grief,
the amount of light in an ending
is greater than the present night.
And what do we do, when a dead man
comes home? Watch Logan's Run,
though I admit I've never seen it,
nor have I seen you return home.

Acknowledgements

This book wouldn't exist if Simon Bodley hadn't saved my life. Everything I write can only exist because Simon was on the scene on October 7th, 2020. Simon, thank you, I owe you more than a few lines in an acknowledgements page.

As always, thanks to Emma, Rue, and Otis, who make everything worth being around for. To Stuart McPherson, Andrew McMillan, Azad Ashim Sharma, James Byrne, Antony Owen, Rob Kiely, Martha Sprackland, Cathleen Allyn Conway, Charlie Baylis, Andre Bagoo, and John Welson for giving their time in friendship, outside of the world of poetry. Thanks to Kashif Sharma-Patel for their work editing this book, and making it a better book.

Some of these poems first appeared in *Anthropocene, Blackbox Manifold, Poetry Wales, Forfatternes Klimaaksjon, Living with Other People,* and *The Last Song: Words for Frightened Rabbit*